THE SPECTACULAR
SUGAR SKULLS
COLORING BOOK

THE SPECTACULAR
SUGAR SKULLS
COLORING BOOK

SIRIUS

This edition published in 2023 by Sirius Publishing, a division of
Arcturus Publishing Limited,
26/27 Bickels Yard, 151–153 Bermondsey Street,
London SE1 3HA

ISBN: 978-1-3988-3124-7
CH011172NT
Supplier 29, Date 1123, Print run 00003867

Printed in China

Introduction

When someone dies, are they really gone? Maybe not, according to the Day of the Dead, a Mexican holiday that welcomes back the souls of deceased loved ones for a family reunion. Sugar skulls, brightly colored and beautifully decorated, are used as an offering and are one of the ways to celebrate the souls and their lives on that holiday. This selection of sugar skulls offers a fabulous range of designs, including different shaped and sized skulls, and a variety of elaborate patterns, allowing you to color in your skulls in your chosen way, just as those celebrating their ancestors do. Whether you celebrate the Day of the Dead or are an admirer of the beauty of sugar skulls, this collection is perfect for adorning with colors. Chose an image worth celebrating, select colors to match, and spend a couple of hours filling in the pages with the vibrancy of life.

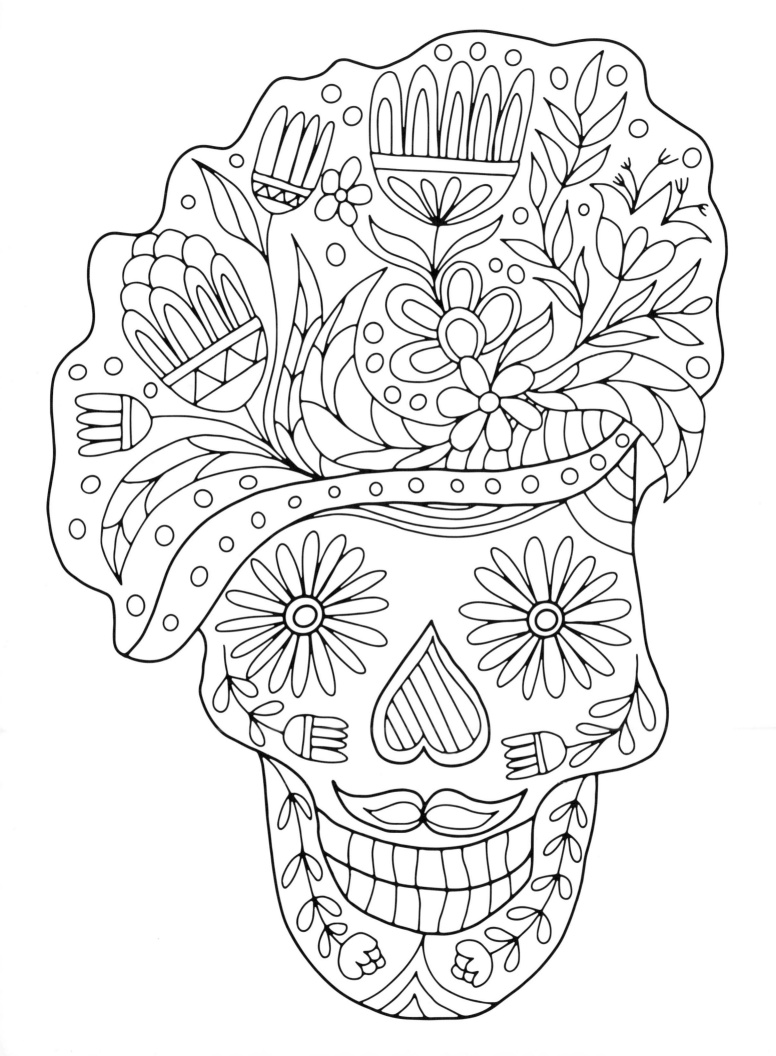

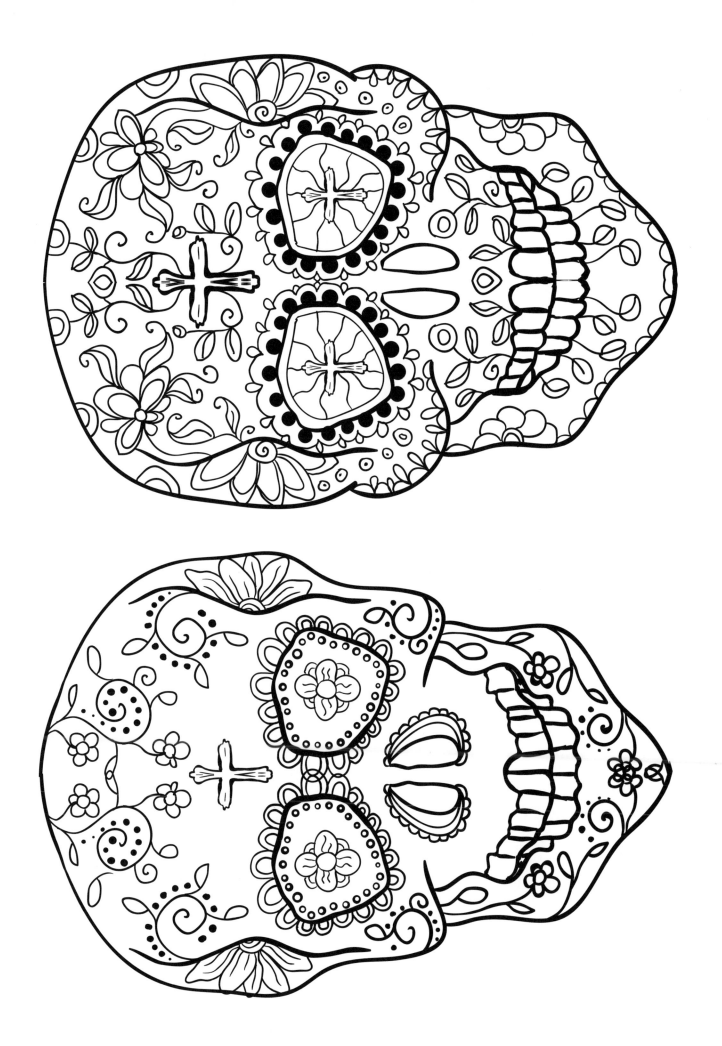